The KIDS' Guide

Dealing With ANXIETY

W
FRANKLIN WATTS
LONDON·SYDNEY

First published in Great Britain in 2022
by Hodder & Stoughton

Copyright © Hodder & Stoughton Limited, 2022
All rights reserved
Editor: Victoria Brooker
Design: Thy Bui
Ilustrator: Scott Garrett

ISBN: 978 1 4451 8281 0 (hbk)
ISBN: 978 1 4451 8282 7 (pbk)
ISBN: 978 1 4451 8743 3 (ebk)

Printed in China

Franklin Watts
An imprint of Hachette Children's Group
Part of Hodder & Stoughton
Carmelite House
50 Victoria Embankment
London EC4Y 0DZ

An Hachette UK Company
www.hachette.co.uk
www.hachettechildrens.co.uk

For information about Sara Stevens and her other books, and for more advice and information, please go to: www.sarastevens.co.uk

INTRODUCTION

Anxiety is when you feel nervous, worried or afraid about a situation or about something happening, such as when it is dark or feeling sick. Sometimes you might feel anxious most of the time, from when you wake until you go to bed.

Anxiety can make you feel nervous about doing things and stop you wanting to take part in activities. You can feel tired, struggle with sleep, fear the future or worry about school and exams.

We all get anxious from time to time and this is quite normal. But if these feelings have started to affect how you live, it's time to find some help. This book will help you to understand what anxiety is, how your mind works and learn ways to help change how you feel.

FEELINGS

We are all different and so anxiety affects us all in different ways. Here are some of the feelings you might have.

Butterflies in the stomach

Loss of appetite

Feeling overwhelmed

Feeling tired and grumpy

Struggling to sleep

Headaches

SO MANY QUESTIONS

You might have lots of questions about anxiety. Here are answers to some common questions. If you have other questions, find someone you trust, such as a teacher, aunt, cousin or carer, to ask more.

Q What is anxiety?

A Anxiety is your body's natural response to stress. It is also called your fight, flight or freeze response.

Q Is anxiety normal?

A Yes, everyone experiences anxiety from time to time.

Q What causes anxiety?

A Getting scared about events or over-worrying about activities such as going to school or doing an exam.

Q Do we all react in the same way to anxiety?

A No, one of your friends might get angry and another might get stomach ache.

Q Will anxiety ever stop?

A Yes, anxiety is like a wave – it builds up then ebbs away. Many people need to ask for help for it to go away.

FIGHT, FLIGHT OR FREEZE

If you think about coming face to face with a scary bear, the three things you might do are:

1

RUN AWAY

2

YELL AND WAVE YOUR ARMS TO SCARE IT AWAY

3

FREEZE IN FEAR.

When we are anxious, we react in one of these three ways and this is called the

fight,

flight

or **freeze**

response. If we bump into a scary bear, then doing one of these things might be a good idea. But worrying about a test at school or about doing something new and reacting in this way is an overreaction, because these are not life or death situations.

Just like a faulty smoke detector that keeps going off for no reason, you might have got your 'fight, flight and freeze' response set to over-respond to the things you get scared about.

Let's look at why your brain does this.

ANXIETY IN YOUR BRAIN

Your brain is like the most amazing computer you could ever find. It is your inner computer, which is sensing, watching and listening 24-hours-a-day to what is happening around you.

Your brain is always ready to leap into action to keep you safe. You might have experienced this when you have been walking downstairs or stepping off a curb – you take a step, but the step is bigger than you'd thought and, in that millisecond, your body reacts setting you right.

The fight, flight or freeze responses instantly switch on. You feel that lurch in your stomach and immediately feel more alert and even anxious. When your brain realises you have found the next step or the ground, all those feelings just switch off again. This is what should happen after the fight, flight or freeze response but sometimes your body doesn't return to normal and this is what anxiety is.

FEEDING THE WORRIES

We all worry from time to time and this is okay. Worry is something we do, for example, when we have to stand up in class and speak in front of others. Having anxiety would be if we feel overwhelmed by these worries. If we worry a lot, our brains begin to hold on to the worries and carry them around, which is what makes anxiety.

Imagine that every worry goes into your own worry cloud that is circling over your head. The more you worry, the bigger, darker and stormier the cloud becomes. You then walk around with the cloud of worries looming over you, following you wherever you go.

You might find that you just can't seem to shake it off and this can make you worry even more and – guess what? – the worry cloud just gets bigger.

When we don't fill the cloud, the cloud doesn't grow and, in fact, something else happens too. The more you forget about worrying, the smaller the worry cloud becomes until, eventually, it just floats away. But how do you stop worrying?

LEARN TO FACE YOUR FEARS

Sometimes we don't want to admit that we are feeling worried or anxious, so we end up feeling unhappy and miserable by pretending everything is okay.

We pretend that we're not worried about all sorts of things, such as being home alone, the fear of dying, embarrassing ourselves in class, being sick, getting bullied, dogs, spiders or even monsters under the bed! We can also worry about teachers telling us off, or about not having done our homework well enough. We hide our worries away by not thinking about them. But deep down, they are still there and we know they are there.

Instead of hiding these worries, we need to stop and face them. We often can't change the things we are trying to hide from so what we need to do is be honest about them. We need to ask for help and learn how to deal with anxious feelings. By asking for help we can get the support we need to face our fears.

EMILY'S STORY

Emily was feeling anxious about going to school. She was scared that someone would be sick and that she would catch the sickness. So she had started not going.

At first, it was just an odd day here and there. She told her parents she didn't feel well. Over time, she had more and more days off from school and people began to notice.

Are you sure there is no one upsetting you or bullying you?

Emily felt under pressure as her parents and friends asked more questions about why she wasn't going to school. It was stressful having to find excuses and say she was feeling ill all the time.

What's wrong?
Where were you yesterday?

AVOIDANCE

Staying at home was not helping Emily. It was just making her feel more alone and giving her more time to think about the fear that she would get sick at school, which was making those fears grow larger and scarier every day.

The more days Emily had off, the more anxious she felt about going to school. Holding things in and fearing going to school worked in the same way as being chased by a scary bear. The more she worried, the bigger the signals of fight, flight or freeze had become in her mind and body.

I wish I could stop feeling this way.

BREAKING THE CYCLE

Eventually, Emily told her dad why she had been avoiding school. Just speaking to her dad was like popping a big bubble of fear. Emily was able to relax a bit knowing that her family finally knew how she was feeling. Her dad explained that, when he was young, he had been afraid of dogs and had worried about going to the park in case there were any dogs there.

Emily went with her dad to speak to her teachers to explain how scared she was of people vomiting, and her fears that she would be sick herself. With the help of her family, friends and teachers, Emily began to overcome her fears.

Emily now knows that the more you avoid and pretend everything is okay, the bigger your fears will become until your head is full of anxious thoughts. With support, Emily found ways to deal with her feelings.

SPEAK OUT

You are not on your own. Lots of other children and adults feel anxiety, so don't be scared to speak out and ask for help. You can talk to your parents, teachers, other staff at school, or to your friends and extended family. You will feel so much better not carrying the worries around on your own. Fears feel much worse just swimming round in your head.

If you are finding it hard to speak to someone, you could write a letter explaining how you feel and what is bothering you. You don't have to let anyone else read the letter if you don't want to. This is just a way to help you start to express how you are feeling.

Read the letter back to yourself and imagine that it is from a friend. Think about what advice you would give to them.

THINGS TO DO WHEN FEELING ANXIOUS

The following pages contain some ideas for things you can do to help with anxiety.

When your brain begins to fill with worries, you can start to feel anxious. Distracting your brain away from the worries can help to reduce them and help you to feel less anxious, too.

Here are a few ideas for how to do this:

1. Spell words backwards in your head. If you're with friends or family, ask each other to spell words backwards. See who can do it the fastest.

2. Get a piece of paper and rip into many pieces. The ripping is distracting and also releases stress.

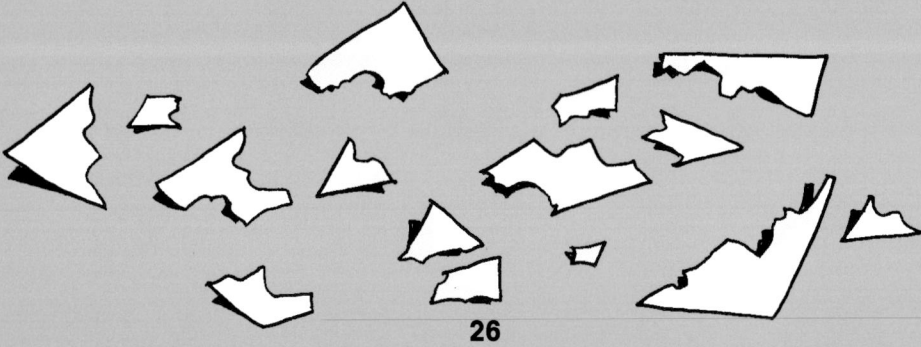

3. Ask for a hug from someone who cares about you and then ask them to talk with you to help distract you from your worries.

4. Pick a letter of the alphabet and think of first names that begin with that letter. You can play this yourself or with friends and family.

5. If you're on a car journey, pick a colour and count how many cars of that colour you see. This is also great to do with the people travelling with you. The first person to spot ten cars of their chosen colour is the winner.

FINGER BREATHING

This is a great activity to help distract yourself from worrying thoughts and to help you to relax.

1. **Stretch one hand out like a star.**

2. **Get the pointer finger of your other hand ready to trace your fingers up and down.**

3. **Slide your pointer finger slow up each finger and slowly down the other side.**

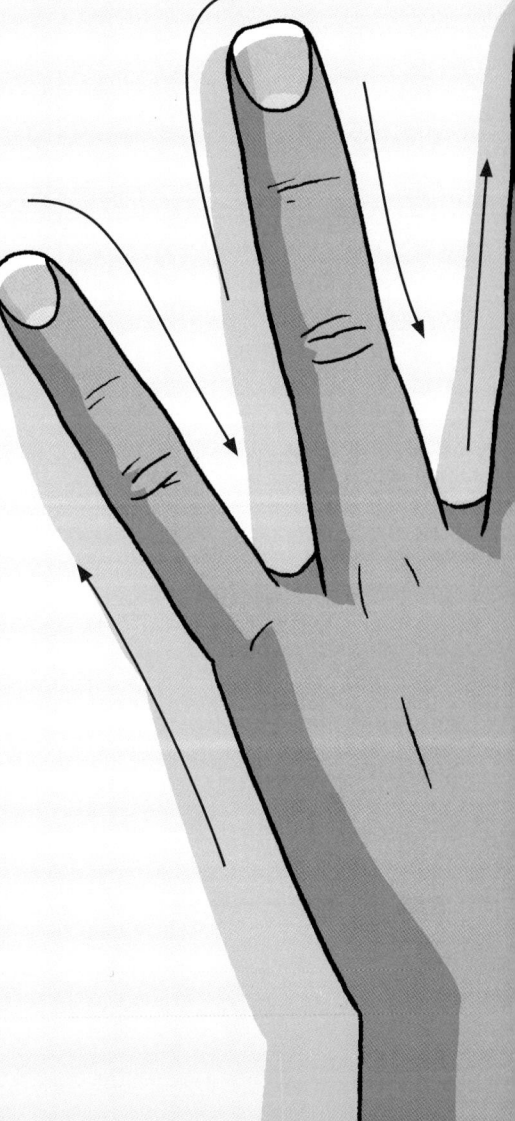

4. As you slide your finger up, breathe in.

5. Breathe out slowly as you slide your finger down.

6. Breathe in and out slowly as you move up and down each finger.

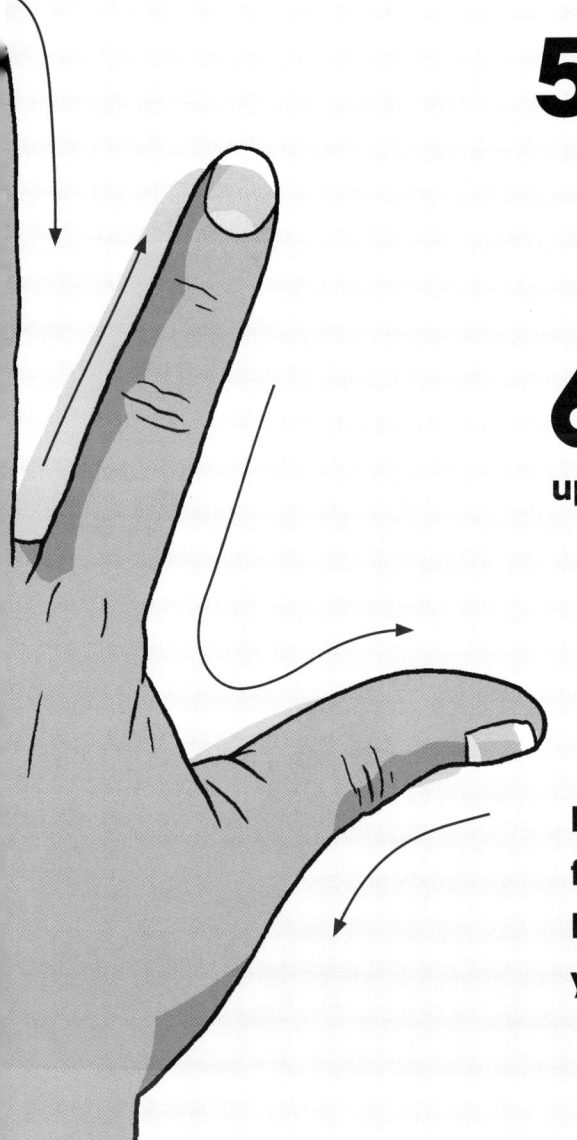

Keep going until you have finished tracing your hand. Repeat on the same hand if you need to or swap hands.

RELAXATION AND BREATHING

Focusing on yourself and your breathing is a good way to help you relax. Try this exercise after school or just before you go to sleep at night.

1. Lie down somewhere comfortable and close your eyes.

2. Place your hands on your stomach and feel your stomach move up and down as you breathe.

3. Each time you breathe, feel your stomach move up and down. Say 'one elephant' as you breathe in and 'two elephants' as you breathe out. Try and do this for ten breaths in and out.

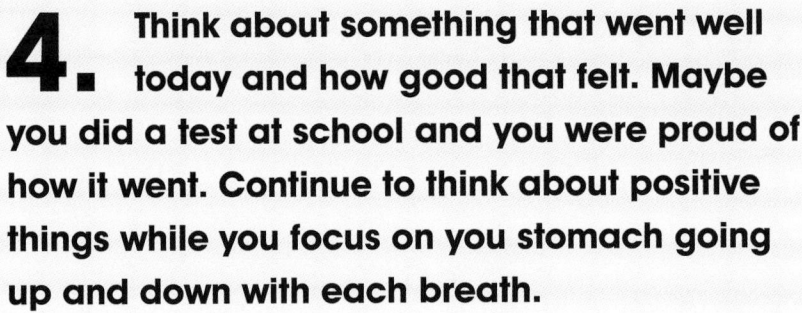

4. Think about something that went well today and how good that felt. Maybe you did a test at school and you were proud of how it went. Continue to think about positive things while you focus on you stomach going up and down with each breath.

5. Now think about something that makes you smile, such as playing with your pet.

6. Finally, while still feeling your stomach go up and down, think about someone who makes you feel good about yourself.

You should now feel more relaxed, calm and happier.

HAVE A POSITIVE MINDSET

Every day is different. Some days will be boring or stressful, but others will be fun or calm. Everyone experiences ups and downs. Try not to be afraid of the bad days and remember that they will pass and good days will come.

Take some time to celebrate the good days and focus on the positives. Call up these positive feelings and memories when you are worrying or feeling stressed to help distract you and create a positive mindset. Every positive thought you have will help you to feel better about yourself. Also, if you are thinking about positive things, you won't have space in your mind to worry about the negative things!

Nobody is perfect so don't set too high expectations for yourself. We all fail at things or make mistakes, even adults. It's part of learning and growing. If we don't get things wrong sometimes, we'll never improve.

MAKE A PLAN

Making a plan is a great way to help ease anxiety and you can use this for lots of different worries and fears you might be having. Maybe you are worried that you won't be picked up from an after-school club. Talk to your parents or carer the night before. Find out who is coming to pick you up from school, discuss what time you need picking up and where from.

You can also make a back-up plan. You can add to your plan that one of your grandparents could pick you up as they are not far away or that one of your friend's mum lives nearby and they could take you to their house. Write down any phone numbers you need. You could also go back into the club to ask an adult for help.

Write your plan down in a notebook so you can take it with you when you go out. Then you can remind yourself about what was agreed if you are feeling anxious.

BUILD YOUR CONFIDENCE

Confidence is not something we are born with; it is a learned habit. We are all born not knowing how to walk, run, talk or write. But we start to learn these skills and the more we practise, the better we become. Of course, in the beginning we must put effort into learning new skills, whether it be walking or running, or learning how to spell, cook, paint, sing or play a video game.

It's important to not let the things we don't get right first time bother us and it is time to say

NO

to those negative thoughts. The more positive we are about things, the better we will feel about ourselves and the more confident we will feel inside.

Sometimes people, situations or even ourselves can be negative, for example, when we are criticised for making a mistake or told off for doing something wrong. Don't dwell on these things, just say sorry if you need to and move on. Always remember the things you get wrong are just a tiny part of who you are; you have lots more things you are good at and do get right. Stay positive and try again.

REASSURANCE

When we feel anxious, we often ask for reassurance.

> Will I be OK, Mum?

> Will I feel anxious at school tomorrow, Aunty?

We also search for reassurance by thinking things like, "If I can't sit next to my best friend then I won't feel safe" or "If my dad can't pick me up from school, then I will be scared".

Choose to flip these negative statements to positive ones. Instead, think: "If I can't sit next to my friend, I will be okay" or "If my dad can't pick me up, I will feel fine going home with my friend's mum". Look for alternatives to reassure yourself rather than looking to others for reassurance. The more you do this, the more confidence in yourself you will gain.

Soon you won't need to search for as much reassurance from your parents and teachers. Your confidence will grow and you will have fewer worries and feel less anxious.

CHALLENGE LISTS

Try doing this activity. It will help to build your confidence and boost your self-esteem, which will help to lessen your anxiety.

Make three lists labelled A, B and C.

A LIST

This lists all the things you can do, such as:

I can do a spelling test at home.

I can chat with a friend.

I can do my homework on time.

B LIST

This lists everything you feel nervous about doing, such as:

I'm scared to speak up in class.

I get anxious at the thought of doing weekly tests at school.

C LIST

This lists all the things you'd like to do, but you don't feel able to try just yet.

I would like to feel able to go out in a big group of friends.

I would like to feel confident about sitting an exam.

You know you can do all the A-list things so now it is time to challenge yourself.

CHALLENGE LISTS STEP BY STEP

Take small steps towards achieving some of the activities on your B-list. If you want to face fears about speaking in front of the class, practise by standing and reading your work out loud to your family. You can also ask if you can start doing your reading with just your teacher first to build your confidence to speak out in front of people.

Try to practise your B-list activities as much as you can and, when these start to feel okay, you can add them to your A-list. Then you move on to the other things on your B-list. Over time, your C-list will also start to seem easier and you can move those actions into the B- or A-lists.

Taking steady and consistent steps is the best way to change. BIG changes start with SMALL steps. Keep finding other small steps that you can take to help you move slowly towards overcoming your fears.

JOURNAL POSITIVES

Take each day as it comes knowing that there are always ups and downs. Try not to be afraid of the bad days and celebrate the good ones. Everyone gets a bit worried or anxious from time to time but now you know some ways to deal with these feelings.

Keep a positivity journal and write in all the new achievements you have made and the positive things people have said to you. Add pictures and photos. Write something every day even if it just a small thing. The little things we do are just as important as the big things.

Over time your journal will become full of wonderful achievements and fun memories. Then, if you're having a bad day, pick up your journal and flick through the pages reminding yourself of all the progress you've made.

It's great to look at your progress. Sometimes just doing one new thing a day doesn't seem much, but fast forward a month, or a few months, and you'll surprise yourself by how far you've come. Some days might be harder than others but keep making small steps towards a HAPPIER, more POSITIVE, you.

FURTHER INFORMATION

Helplines – You can use a helpline if you want to talk to someone about how you're feeling. Trained staff and volunteers will listen to you, and offer advice.

You can call Childline for free on 0800 1111. They also have a great website full of helpful advice as well as fun things to do: www.childline.org.uk/kids.

Counsellors – If you don't feel comfortable talking to people you know about your feelings, you could try and see a counsellor. Speaking in private to someone separate from your home life can be very useful.

Journals – Writing in a journal can help when things get too much. All you need to do is get hold of a blank notebook and jot down how you feel. Putting your emotions on paper can be a good way of getting them out of your head, and helping you understand them.

For further advice and information, please take a look at the author's websites:
www.sarastevens.co.uk
https://saramindhealth.co.uk/

BOOKS TO READ

Be Your Best You: How to manage your mental health, your time on social media and beat stress and anxiety
by Honor Head (Franklin Watts, 2021)

Build Resilience: Anxiety and Self-Esteem
by Honor Head (Franklin Watts, 2019)

Don't Feed The Cat;
The Cat Is Back;
I Can't See The Cat
by Sara Stevens (Sara Stevens, 2020)

Keep Your Cool: How to Deal with Life's Worries and Stress
by Dr Aaron Balick (Franklin Watts, 2020)

The Worry (Less) Book: Feel Strong, Find Calm and Tame Your Anxiety
by Rachel Brian (Wren and Rook, 2020)

Your Mind Matters: Beating Stress and Anxiety
by Honor Head (Franklin Watts, 2019)

INDEX

anger 7, 9
appetite 6

brains 11, 12, 13, 14, 26,
breathing exercises 28–29, 30–31

challenges 40, 41, 42, 43
confidence 36, 37, 39, 40, 42

distraction techniques 26, 27, 28–29, 30–31, 32
dogs 16, 22

exams 4, 9, 41

failure 33
family 22, 24, 26, 27, 42
fear 4, 7, 9, 10, 17
fears 16, 17, 18, 20, 21, 23, 24, 25, 34, 42, 43
fight, flight, freeze response 8, 10–11, 13, 21
friends 9, 19, 22, 24, 25, 26, 27, 40, 41

grumpiness 6

headaches 6
help 4, 9, 17, 22, 24, 35
homework 16, 40

journals 44, 45

letter writing 25

nervousness 4, 41

overreactions 11

parents 18, 19, 22, 24, 34, 39, 42
planning 34, 35, 42
positive mindset 32, 33

reassurance 38–39

school 4, 9, 11, 16, 18, 20, 21, 24, 30, 34, 35, 41
self-esteem 40
sickness (feeling sick/ stomach ache) 4, 9, 16, 18, 19, 20, 21, 22
sleep 4, 6, 30
stomach 6, 9, 13, 21, 30, 31

stress 8, 19, 26, 32

teachers 8, 16, 18, 22, 24, 39, 42
tiredness 4, 6

worries 4, 9, 14–15, 16, 23, 24, 25, 26, 27, 28, 34, 39